101 Awesome Bible Facts for Kids

Sandy Silverthorne

HARVEST HOUSE PUBLISHERS

EUGENE, OREGON

Cover by Left Coast Design, Portland, Oregon

101 AWESOME BIBLE FACTS FOR KIDS
Copyright © 2010 by Sandy Silverthorne
Published by Harvest House Publishers
Eugene, Oregon 97402
www.harvesthousepublishers.com

ISBN 978-0-7369-2926-4

Printed in the United States of America

12 13 14 15 16 17 18 / BP-SK / 10 9 8 7 6 5 4 3

Introduction

Q: How big was Noah's Ark?
A: About 450 feet long.

Q: How did conquering armies get over walled cities?
A: With siege mounds.

Q: How much could Samson bench press?
A: Okay, we couldn't figure that one out, but we
   know the dude was strong.

Welcome to *101 Awesome Bible Facts for Kids!* The
Bible is full of amazing stories, characters, and
events, and this little book will help you get up close
and personal with many of them. You're going to
find out things you never dreamed of, like which
book of the Bible never mentions God, how much
a pyramid weighs, and whether or not David really
could defeat Goliath with just a sling and a stone. In
addition, every few pages you'll come across some
extra features:

- *Bible Bonuses* are little-known facts that
  will astound you and your friends.

- *Word 4 Word* items will help you
  understand the original Greek or Hebrew
  meaning of some of the common words in
  the Bible.

- On the ever popular *Catch Phrase* pages,
  you'll discover that some phrases that
  we use every day actually come from the
  Bible!

You might enjoy reading *101 Awesome Bible Facts
for Kids* in one sitting, or you could use it as a daily
devotional. Each day, read one fact and then look up
the Scripture at the bottom of the page to see what
God's Word is telling you. Either way, have fun and
get ready to learn some awesome stuff from the
original awesome book—the Bible.

1 WHAT WAS THE FORBIDDEN FRUIT?

Most people assume the fruit was an apple, but the Bible never tells us what it was. The fruit could have been a peach or even a pomegranate. The important thing to remember is that God said not to eat it, and Adam and Eve disobeyed.

The woman said to the serpent, "We may eat the fruit of the trees of the garden; but of the fruit of the tree which is in the midst of the garden, God has said, 'You shall not eat it'" (Genesis 3:2-3).

2 ADAM = MAN = DiRT

Adam's name comes from the Hebrew word *a da ma*, which means "the ground." When God made Adam, He used many of the earth's elements, including hydrogen and oxygen. Hydrogen and oxygen make water, and water makes up more than half your body weight.

Then the LORD God took the man [a da ma] and put him in the Garden of Eden to tend it and keep it (Genesis 2:15).

3 WHERE WAS THE GARDEN OF EDEN?

The Bible mentions four rivers near the garden. You can still find two of these rivers on maps today—the Euphrates and the Tigris. Check it out. They flow into the Persian Gulf on either side of Iraq.

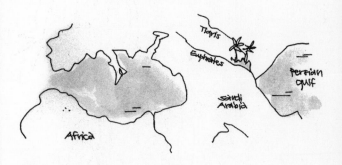

The name of the third river is Tigris; it flows east of Assyria. And the fourth river is the Euphrates (Genesis 2:14 NASB).

4 NOAH AND THE ARK

The Bible says that every kind of animal was on the ark. There were members of the cat species (like lions or tigers) and members of the dog species (like wolves), but not every member of the species had to be on board.

Of the birds after their kind, of animals after their kind, and of every creeping thing of the earth after its kind, two of every kind will come to you to keep them alive (Genesis 6:20).

BIBLE BONUS:
How Long Is a Cubit?

You're going to need this information in some of the upcoming pages. In Bible times, people measured things by cubits, just as we measure in feet and yards. Some people think a cubit was about 18 inches long. So if something was 10 cubits long, it would be about 180 inches, or 15 feet. Others, however, think the cubit was 21 inches.

5 HOW BIG WAS THE ARK?

According to Genesis 6:15, the ark was at least 450 feet long, 75 feet wide, and 45 feet high. That's about half the size of an aircraft carrier. Aircraft carriers are more than 1000 feet long and can carry 5000 people and 90 planes. According to some scholars, Noah's ark could hold as much cargo as 330 railroad cars!

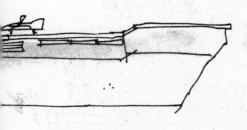

And this is how you shall make it: The length of the ark shall be three hundred cubits, its width fifty cubits, and its height thirty cubits (Genesis 6:15).

WORD 4 WORD:
Abundantly (Greek, *perissos*)

This word describes something that is overflowing, excessive, surplus, over and above, or more than sufficient. So in John 10:10, when Jesus says He's come to give us life abundantly, He means the life He has for us is superabundant.

6 ARE WE THERE YET?

How long were Noah & Company inside the ark? Most people think they were inside 40 days and 40 nights because that's how long the rain fell (Genesis 7:12). But Noah's family and all the animals were actually in the ark for a year and ten days. They went in when Noah was 599 years, 1 month, and 17 days old. They came out when Noah was 600 years, 1 month, and 27 days old.

In the six hundredth year of Noah's life, in the second month, the seventeenth day of the month, on that day all the fountains of the great deep were broken up, and the windows of heaven were opened…

And it came to pass on the six hundred and first year…in the second month, on the twenty-seventh day of the month, the earth was dried (Genesis 7:11; 8:13-14).

7 HAPPY LANDING

The Bible tells us that Noah's ark finally
rested on Mount Ararat (in southern Asia).
Mount Ararat still stands near the borders of
Iran and Armenia. Many people believe that
the ark or its remains still reside up there.

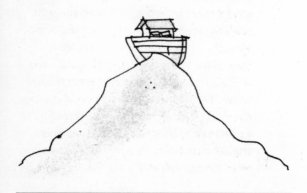

*Then the ark rested in the seventh month, the seventeenth
day of the month, on the mountains of Ararat (Genesis 8:4).*

8 MAKE A RAINBOW

God used a rainbow as a sign to Noah that He
would never flood the earth again. That's a
good thing to remember whenever you see a
rainbow in the sky. You can often see a rainbow
when the sun is behind you and the air in
front of you is filled with mist. Drops of water
act like prisms and separate the sunlight into
colors. If you want to make your own rainbow,
stand with your back to the sun and spray
a mist from a garden hose into the air. This
works best in the morning or late afternoon,
when the sun isn't straight above you.

*I set My rainbow in the cloud, and it shall be for the sign of
the covenant between Me and the earth (Genesis 9:13).*

9 THE TOWER OF BABEL

When we think of a
tower, we usually think
of something tall
and straight like the
Empire State
Building in New
York City. But the
Tower of Babel was
probably built in the
shape of a stair-
stepped pyramid,
called a ziggurat.
The tallest known
ziggurat was about
300 feet high. That's
pretty tall, but
hardly as high as
heaven. In fact,
the Empire State
Building is
1250 feet tall!

Heaven

← Empire
State
Building

ziggurat

---

*And they said, "Come, let us build ourselves a city, and a
tower whose top is in the heavens; let us make a name for
ourselves" (Genesis 11:4).*

WORD 4 WORD:
One Accord (Greek, homothumadan)

This Greek word describes a group of people who all agree on something important. In Acts 2:1 it describes Jesus' disciples being in agreement in the upper room on the day of Pentecost.

10 PASS THE SLIME

To build the Tower of Babel, clay bricks were stacked on top of one another and held together with asphalt. Asphalt is that black sticky tar that's been around since the Bible times and is still used in building roads today. Older versions of the Bible refer to it as "slime."

They had brick for stone, and they had asphalt [slime] for mortar (Genesis 11:3).

11   HOW DO YOU SAY...?

Before the Tower of Babel, the whole earth
spoke one language. Today there are more
than 3000 different languages in the world.
One of the most interesting is Silbo Gomero,
a language that is whistled instead of spoken.

---

*Therefore its name is called Babel [confusion], because
there the LORD confused the language of all the earth
(Genesis 11:9).*

12 BIG-CITY BLUES

When God called Abram's family to leave the city of Ur, they had to leave behind a beautiful, sophisticated city of more than a quarter of a million people. Ur was one of the oldest cities on earth and was an extremely wealthy shipping center. It even had canals.

And Terah took his son Abram and his grandson Lot, the son of Haran, and his daughter-in-law Sarai, his son Abram's wife, and they went out with them from Ur of the Chaldeans (Genesis 11:31).

CATCHPHRASE:
The Apple of My Eye

If you are the apple of someone's eye, you are very special to that person. God called Israel the apple of His eye in Deuteronomy 32:10. He loves Israel, and He loves you too.

13 MORE THAN THE STARS

God promised Abram that his children,
grandchildren, and great-great-great grandchildren would number more than the stars
in the sky. Currently we can see about 3000
stars at night, but more than 18 million
Jewish people are living today. God's promise
came through!

---

*"Look now toward heaven, and count the stars if you are
able to number them." And He said to him, "So shall your
descendants be"* (Genesis 15:5).

14 THE FERTILE CRESCENT

After Abram left Ur, he traveled along the
Euphrates River to Haran and then later to
the land of Canaan. This route followed an
area we call the Fertile Crescent because
things grow well there and because it is
shaped like a crescent moon. By following
this route, Abram's party always had plenty
of water as well as vegetation to eat.

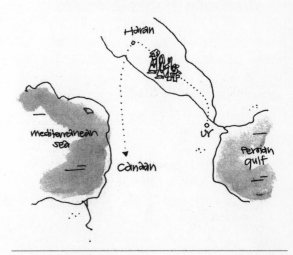

*So Abram departed as the LORD had spoken to him, and
Lot went with him. And Abram was seventy-five years old
when he departed from Haran (Genesis 12:4).*

WORD 4 WORD:
Almighty (Hebrew, *shaddai*)

The Hebrew word *shaddai* means "all-powerful." Sometimes God is referred to as *El-Shaddai*, which means "God Almighty" (Genesis 17:1). It describes one who is great, strong, everlasting, and all-sufficient.

15 TRAVELING COMPANIONS

Abraham may have started raising camels
while he was in Egypt. Camels were faster
than donkeys, and they could carry at least
400 pounds. They could also go for days
without water. There was one problem,
though. They constantly swayed back and
forth, so you could get really
seasick riding one.

---

*He had sheep, oxen, male donkeys, male and female
servants, female donkeys, and camels (Genesis 12:16).*

16 A TRUSTING SON

Isaac was probably between 16 and 25 years old when God asked his 100-year-old father to sacrifice him. Isaac could have easily escaped, but apparently he trusted God and his dad. God came through at the very last minute by providing a ram as a substitute for the sacrifice.

And Abraham said, "My son, God will provide for Himself the lamb for a burnt offering." So the two of them went together (Genesis 22:8).

17 WHAT'S IN A NAME?
PART 1: JACOB THE SUPPLANTER

When Isaac and Rebekah had twin boys, they named one of them Jacob. The name meant "supplanter" or "holding onto the heel"—wrestling terms for gaining the advantage over an opponent. Jacob spent most of his life doing just that, trying to gain the advantage over his twin brother, Esau.

Afterward his brother came out, and his hand took hold of Esau's heel; so his name was called Jacob (Genesis 25:26).

WHAT'S IN A NAME? PART 2: HAIRY ESAU

Isaac and Rebekah's other son was named Esau, which means "hairy." He loved being outdoors and was a skillful hunter. Rebekah loved Jacob, and Isaac loved Esau. That's when things started to unravel.

And the first came out red. He was like a hairy garment all over; so they called his name Esau (Genesis 25:25).

19 BIRTHRIGHT STEW

One day, Jacob was cooking up some yummy red stew. When Esau came in from hunting and smelled the delicious aroma, he begged Jacob to give him some. Jacob said, "If you'll give me your birthright (the privilege of being the firstborn), I'll give you some stew." In those days, the firstborn received a bigger inheritance and a lot of honor. Esau agreed to Jacob's trade, and Jacob had pulled one over on his brother.

And Jacob gave Esau bread and stew of lentils; then he ate and drank, arose, and went his way. Thus Esau despised his birthright (Genesis 25:34).

WORD 4 WORD:
Believe (Greek, aman)

This word means to be convinced of something in a firm, stable, and established way. It can also mean to be firmly persuaded. When we say amen after we say a prayer, we're asking that the requests we made to God may be solidly and firmly established.

20 NEW NAME, NEW PERSON

After Jacob stole Esau's birthright and his blessing from their father, he fled to Haran, where some of his family still lived. After many years of hiding out, Jacob returned to see his brother again. On the way back,

Jacob spent the night wrestling with an angel, who gave Jacob a new name. Instead of Jacob—"grabbing the heel"—his name would now be Israel—"God's Fighter" or "Prince with God." From then on Jacob (or Israel) fought for God and not against Him.

And He said, "Your name shall no longer be called Jacob, but Israel; for you have struggled with God and with men, and have prevailed" (Genesis 32:28).

21 NICE THREADS

Jacob finally settled down and had 12 sons and a daughter. Joseph was his dad's favorite, and his dad gave him a coat with many colors on it. The original language could mean that the coat was long sleeved. In Joseph's day, people who did the heavy work wore tunics that had short sleeves or no sleeves at all. Long-sleeved tunics were for people who didn't have to work hard. This could have been another reason Joseph's brothers didn't like him.

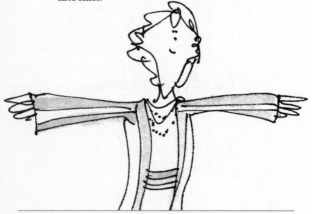

Now Israel loved Joseph more than all his children, because he was the son of his old age. Also he made him a tunic of many colors (Genesis 37:3).

22 FOR SALE–CHEAP!

When Jacob's sons met a caravan of traders from Midian, they saw their chance to make some money and get rid of their little brother at the same time. They sold Joseph as a slave to the Midianites for 20 shekels of silver—less than $50 today.

So the brothers pulled Joseph up and lifted him out of the pit, and sold him to the Ishmaelites for twenty shekels of silver (Genesis 37:28).

23 PYRAMID BUILDING

Pyramids were a familiar sight to Joseph. But pyramid building was in fashion for only 200 or 300 years. The pyramids that Joseph saw had been standing for a thousand years by the time he arrived in Egypt.

Now the Midianites had sold him in Egypt to Potiphar, an officer of Pharaoh and captain of the guard (Genesis 37:36).

24 HEAVY-DUTY

The Great Pyramid of Giza is built with
2.5 million blocks of stone. This pyramid
weighed in at about 5 billion pounds!

*The LORD was with Joseph, and he was a successful
man; and he was in the house of his master the Egyptian
(Genesis 39:2).*

WORD 4 WORD:
Cheerful (Greek, *hilaros*)

This word describes someone who is willing, good-natured, and joyfully ready. When Paul asks the Corinthians to be cheerful givers in 2 Corinthians 9:7, he means that they should give with a joyful willingness. Look at the word again. Does it look a little like a modern word? The English word *hilarious* comes from this root.

26 MOSES' EDUCATION

Moses was adopted by Pharaoh's daughter while he was still an infant. In Pharaoh's palace, Moses received a prince's education. Princes were taught geometry, poetry, and astronomy. They learned to write in hieroglyphics as well as other languages. Not many people knew how to write in those days, but God was preparing Moses to write the first five books of the Bible.

And the child grew, and she brought him to Pharaoh's daughter, and he became her son. So she called his name Moses (Exodus 2:10).

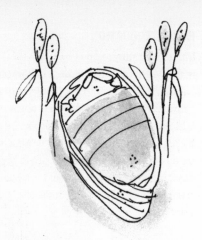

27 ARK NUMBER 2

In order to save Moses' life, his mother put him in a little basket and placed him in the Nile River. The word used for Moses' little watertight boat is the same word used for the ark Noah built. It refers to a floating vessel. Both arks were used to save a race of people but in very different ways!

But when she could no longer hide him, she took an ark of bulrushes for him, daubed it with asphalt and pitch, put the child in it, and laid it in the reeds by the river's bank (Exodus 2:3).

28 PAPYRUS

We usually think that the bulrushes used to make Moses' boat were like little cattails, but they weren't. The three-sided reeds grew up to 16 feet tall and 3 inches across. Egyptians discovered how to make these plants into rolls of paper that sometimes stretched 120 feet long!

When she saw the ark among the reeds, she sent her maid to get it (Exodus 2:5).

THE TEN PLAGUES

During Moses' time, the Egyptians worshipped many parts of creation as if they were gods—the river, the sun, the sky, and even the crops. The ten plagues that God sent on the Egyptians proved to Pharaoh that the living God was more powerful than all of their so-called gods (Exodus 12:12).

BLOOD

God's first sign was to turn the Nile River into blood. The Nile was the main source of water and irrigation for the whole country, and the Egyptians believed it was a god.

FROGS

God sent so many frogs that they were in all the people's beds, in their kitchens, and even in their ovens! The Egyptians worshipped a goddess of fertility named Heqt, who had the head and body of a frog.

GNATS

These were tiny little fleas that literally got under everyone's skin. God commanded Aaron to "strike the dust of the land" and cause the gnats to rise up (Exodus 8:16), so this plague was a direct affront to the Egyptians' god of the earth.

FLIES

This swarm might have been gadflies that bite or sting—flies that attach to the body. God's people, the Jews, were kept safe from this and all the other plagues.

LIVESTOCK

All the livestock that belonged to the Egyptians died during this plague, which confronted Hathor, the mother-goddess of Egypt, who resembled a cow.

BOILS

These burning, raised bumps on the Egyptians' skin were so painful that Pharaoh's magicians couldn't even stand up! This plague might have been an attack on the Egyptians' god of medicine.

HAIL

This supernatural hailstorm was mixed with fire. The subsequent destruction of the crops insulted Isis, the Egyptian goddess of life, whose job was to protect them.

LOCUSTS

These large grasshoppers could (and still can) strip a land of all its crops in a matter of hours. This plague once again confronted the Egyptian gods Isis and Seth, who were supposed to protect the land.

DARKNESS

This plague was important because the most powerful god in Egypt was the sun god, Ra. Pharaoh was supposed to be a human version of this god.

DEATH OF THE FiRSTBORN

Only the Jews and a few God-fearing Egyptians who followed God's command to brush a lamb's blood over the doorposts of their houses escaped this plague. According to Exodus 12:12, this plague was directed against all the gods of Egypt.

29 ROLL CALL

When God used Moses to lead His people out of Egypt, 600,000 men left with him. Their wives and children went too, so about 2.5 to 3 million people followed Moses. If all those who left stood in a line, they would stretch from Egypt to the Promised Land and back!

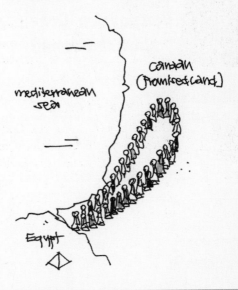

Then the children of Israel journeyed from Rameses to Succoth, about six hundred thousand men on foot, besides children (Exodus 12:37).

WORD 4 WORD:
Compassion (Greek, splanchnizomai)

This Greek word describes deep compassion (Matthew 9:36). In Greek, the *splanchna* was the very inside of a person, where people believed strong emotions came from. It's like saying you've got a strong feeling in your gut.

30 WHAT IS IT?

God miraculously fed all the Jewish people in
the desert. Every morning a white substance
appeared on the ground. At first the Israelites
didn't know what the small flakes that looked
like frost were. So they named it *manna*,
which literally means "What is it?" in the
Hebrew language. God fed His people with
manna for 40 years as they wandered in the
wilderness.

*So when the children of Israel saw it, they said to one
another, "What is it?" For they did not know what it was*
(Exodus 16:15).

31 HOW MANY TABLETS?

God gave Moses the Ten Commandments on Mount Sinai. They were an agreement between God and His people. In those days, when a strong king made an agreement with a weaker nation, he wrote out two copies of the covenant, one for himself and one for the people. God gave Moses both copies

to show Israel that He was right there with them. When Moses came down the mountain and saw the people worshipping a golden calf, he became so angry that he broke both copies. Later, God wrote two more, so there were four copies of the Ten Commandments.

And the LORD said to Moses, "Cut two tablets of stone like the first ones, and I will write on these tablets the words that were on the first tablets which you broke" (Exodus 34:1).

BiBLE BONUS:
The Five Hairiest Men in the Old Testament

1 Esau—"Esau my brother is a hairy man" (Genesis 27:11). His name even means "hairy."

2 Elijah—"A hairy man wearing a leather belt around his waist" (2 Kings 1:8).

3 Samson—"No razor shall come upon his head" (Judges 13:5). See Awesome Bible Facts 42 and 43.

4 Absalom, David's son—"And when he cut the hair of his head—at the end of every year he cut it because it was heavy on him—when he cut it, he weighed the hair of his head at two hundred shekels" (2 Samuel 14:26). That's about five pounds!

5 Nebuchadnezzer, king of Babylon—"His hair had grown like eagle's feathers" (Daniel 4:33).

THE CONDENSED VERSION

The first four commandments have to do with our relationship with God. He knows it's not good for us to follow anyone or anything else. The last six commandments have to do with the way we treat one another. We shouldn't lie to one another, steal, or murder, and we should always give honor to our parents.

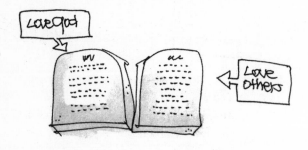

Jesus summed up all the commandments in Mark 12:29-31 when He said we should love God with all our heart, soul, mind, and strength and love people just like we love ourselves.

Teacher, which is the great commandment in the law? (Matthew 22:36).

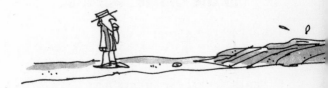

33 THE JORDAN RiVER

After Moses died and Joshua began to lead
the Hebrew people into the Promised Land,
God performed a miracle and opened the
Jordan River so they could cross over, just as
He had opened the Red Sea 40 years earlier. In
1927 a small earthquake caused dirt to block
the Jordan River in just about the same place.
It was stopped up for more than 20 hours!

*Then the priests who bore the ark of the covenant of the
LORD stood firm on dry ground in the midst of the Jordan;
and all Israel crossed over on dry ground (Joshua 3:17).*

BIBLE BONUS:
Four Extremely Bald Men in the Old Testament

1 Samson—"Then [Delilah] lulled him to sleep on her knees, and called for a man and had him shave off the seven locks of his head" (Judges 16:19).

2 Elijah—"As he was going up the road, some youths came from the city and mocked him, and said to him, 'Go up, you baldhead! Go up, you baldhead!'" (2 Kings 2:23).

3 Ezra—"I tore my garment and my robe, and plucked out some of the hair of my head and beard" (Ezra 9:3). Ouch.

4 Job—"Then Job arose, tore his robe, and shaved his head" (Job 1:20).

34 BUILDING BLOCKS

The bricks that the Babylonians used to build the ziggurats were flat and square and baked in ovens. Later, when the Egyptians were involved in building projects, they used bricks that were shaped like rectangles and dried in the sun.

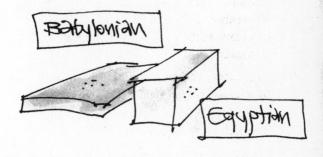

Babylonian

Egyptian

So the Egyptians made the children of Israel serve with rigor. And they made their lives bitter with hard bondage—in mortar, in brick, and in all manner of service in the field. All their service in which they made them serve was with rigor (Exodus 1:13-14).

35 MOSES AND THE BURNING BUSH

One day while Moses was tending the sheep in Midian, he came across a burning bush—

probably a mimosa or thorny acacia tree. A bush on fire in the desert wasn't anything unusual, but something was different about this bush. It was on fire, but it didn't burn up! God spoke to Moses there and started him on his journey to help God free His people from Pharoah.

And the Angel of the Lord appeared to him in a flame of fire from the midst of a bush. So he looked, and behold, the bush was burning with fire, but the bush was not consumed (Exodus 3:2).

WORD 4 WORD:
Example (Greek, *hupogrammos*)

This word combines two Greek words—*hupo*, which means "under," and *grapho*, which means "to write." It originally meant "to trace letters on paper." Then it came to mean "following an example." In 1 Peter 2:21, Peter tells us that we should follow Christ's example.

36 JUDGES

After Joshua died, Israel went into a period of sin and confusion. Without a strong leader like Moses or Joshua, the people did what they thought was right in their own eyes. When they got in trouble, God sent a judge to deliver them. Most of the time these God-appointed leaders were like military generals who led the people against their enemies.

The LORD raised up judges who delivered them out of the hand of those who plundered them (Judges 2:16).

37 AMAZING PROPHECIES

In Bible times, God sometimes gave prophecies to encourage people or to reveal His unfolding plan to bring people back to Himself. More than 100 different prophecies in the Old Testament tell about the coming of Jesus or give specifics about His life and are fulfilled in the New Testament. Here are just a few:

Facts About the Messiah	Old Testament Prediction	New Testament Fulfillment
was born of a virgin	Isaiah 7:14	Luke 1:34
was born in Bethlehem	Micah 5:2	Matthew 2:1
lived in Egypt	Hosea 11:1	Matthew 2:14-15
entered Jerusalem on a donkey	Zechariah 9:9	John 12:14-15
suffered crucifixion	Psalm 22:16-18	Luke 23:33
rose from the dead	Psalm 16:10	Mark 16:6

correct | incorrect

38 GIDEON'S GOOF

To thresh wheat, workers tossed the grain into the air with a pitchfork. The heavy wheat kernels (the good stuff) fell to the ground while the hollow shells or chaff (the bad stuff) blew away.

When the angel found Gideon, he was threshing wheat in a winepress. Wheat is supposed to be threshed on a windy hill, but a winepress is a big hole in the ground used to tread out the grapes. Gideon was hiding from the Midianites, so he chose to hide in the hole.

Gideon threshed wheat in the winepress, in order to hide it from the Midianites (Judges 6:11).

CATCHPHRASE:
A Drop in the Bucket

This phrase signifies a tiny amount compared to something larger. For example, "A hundred dollars is just a drop in the bucket for a multimillionaire." The phrase comes from Isaiah 40:15, where all the nations of the world are considered a drop in the bucket compared to the awesome God of the whole universe.

39 I'M SCARED!

Before Gideon was ready to fight against the Midianites, he needed some encouragement from God, so he laid a sheepskin on the ground. He asked God to make the fleece damp and the ground dry by morning. That's just what happened. Then he asked something like this: "Could we do this again? Only this time, in the morning, could the fleece be dry and the ground wet?" He knew that would really be a miracle because the ground usually dries faster than wool. The next morning, the ground was wet, but the fleece was dry! This was how God encouraged Gideon and showed him that He was with him.

And God did so that night. It was dry on the fleece only, but there was dew on the ground (Judges 6:40).

TRY THIS YOURSELF

Take a wool baseball cap out on the lawn on a sunny day. Wet the cap and the ground and see which one dries first!

trumpet (shofar)

pitcher

torch inside

40 MIDNIGHT SURPRISE

In Gideon's surprise attack, he gave each of his men a trumpet, a torch, and a pitcher. On his signal, each man broke his pitcher, exposing his torch, and at the same time blew his trumpet. Most battles occurred in the daytime on a battlefield, so the Midianites thought they were about to get slaughtered in their tents. They ran in every direction!

Then the three companies blew the trumpets and broke the pitchers—they held the torches in their left hands and the trumpets in their right hands for blowing (Judges 7:20).

WORD 4 WORD:
Faith (Greek, *pistis*)

This word refers to confidence, trust, belief, and trust-worthiness. When Jesus tells His followers to have faith in God in Mark 11:22, He's saying God is worthy of their trust and confidence.

DRUM AND BUGLE CORPS

Armies usually had only one trumpeter for every company of men. When the Midianites heard 300 trumpets, they imagined 300 companies of Israelite soldiers surrounding them! They thought they were majorly outnumbered!

When the three hundred blew the trumpets, the LORD set every man's sword against his companion throughout the whole camp, and the army fled (Judges 7:22).

42 SAMSON'S STATS

Team: the Zorah Nazirites

Age drafted: before birth

Agent: an angel

Age called up to the big leagues: 20

Years in the pros (judging Israel): 20

Position: pitcher

Total strikeouts: more than 4000

Batting average: 1000

Favorite bat: donkey's jawbone

Primary strength: hair

Primary weakness: Delilah

I have been a Nazirite to God from my mother's womb. If I am shaven, then my strength will leave me, and I shall become weak, and be like any other man (Judges 16:17).

43 WHAT WAS A NAZIRITE?

In Old Testament times, several people were called to take a Nazirite vow. This signified that they were set apart for God in a special way. The vow included three things: no drinking alcohol, no touching dead stuff, and never cutting their hair. Some guys took this vow for a limited time, but Samson appeared to see it as a lifelong agreement. Unfortunately, Samson evidently violated his vow, and that led to his problems. In the New Testament, John the Baptist may have been a Nazirite.

For behold, you shall conceive and bear a son. And no razor shall come upon his head, for the child shall be a Nazirite to God from the womb (Judges 13:5).

44 CUTTING CORNERS

In Leviticus 19:9-10, God commands His people to harvest only the middle portion of their property. That way the poor could come and gather or "glean" what was left over. This was an early way of making sure that all the people had a way to provide for themselves and their families. And that's what Ruth was doing when she met Boaz.

And you shall not glean your vineyard, nor shall you gather every grape of your vineyard; you shall leave them for the poor and the stranger; I am the LORD your God (Leviticus 19:10).

WORD 4 WORD:
God (Hebrew, *Elohim*)

This word appears more than 2500 times in the Old Testament. It means "God," "God in His fullness," and oftentimes "God the Creator." It's used in the very first verse of the Bible "In the beginning God…"

45 KINSMAN-REDEEMER

In Ruth's day, when a husband died, God had a plan to take care of the wife. He commanded the man's brother (or nearest relative) to marry and support the widowed woman. This man was called the kinsman-redeemer. Boaz was a relative of Elimelech, Ruth's late husband, so Boaz acted as Ruth's kinsman-redeemer. This was an early picture of what Jesus has done for us by bringing us into His family.

This man is a relation of ours, one of our close relatives (Ruth 2:20).

46 RUTH—GRANDMOTHER TO A KING

Even though Ruth was not an Israelite, she married Boaz and became the great-grandmother of King David. That means she became part of the royal bloodline that led to Jesus. Check it out in Matthew 1. This shows that God welcomes all who want to join His family, regardless of their background.

Salmon begot Boaz, and Boaz begot Obed; Obed begot Jesse, and Jesse begot David (Ruth 4:21-22).

47 LEGAL SANDALRY

In Ruth 4:7-8, Ruth's relative gives his sandal to Boaz as a way to seal the agreement for Boaz to marry Ruth. In ancient Israel, giving your sandal to another person was a way of making the agreement legal. This custom may have gone way back to when God promised His people, "Every place on which the soul of your foot treads shall be yours" (Deuteronomy 11:24).

Now this was the custom in former times in Israel concerning redeeming and exchanging, to confirm anything: one man took off his sandal and gave it to the other (Ruth 4:7).

48 BATTLE PLANS, PART 1: A BIG-TICKET ITEM

When a nation had chariots for warfare, they really had an advantage. But chariots weren't cheap. A chariot was worth more than a man. Joseph was sold into slavery for only 20 shekels of silver (Genesis 37:28), but 600 years later, King Solomon paid more than 600 shekels—about $1300 today—for each of his 1400 chariots!

They also acquired and imported from Egypt a chariot for six hundred shekels of silver, and a horse for one hundred and fifty (2 Chronicles 1:17).

49 BATTLE PLANS, PART 2: ALL AQUIVER

A quiver, the pouch that held an archer's arrows, held about 30 arrows. Arrows from Old Testament times have been found with their owners' names on them!

Like arrows in the hand of a warrior, so are the children of one's youth. Happy is the man who has his quiver full of them (Psalm 127:4-5).

WORD 4 WORD:
Grace (Greek, *charis*)

This word refers to unearned favor and undeserved blessing. It's the word that describes God's great love and favor toward us even when we don't deserve it (Ephesians 2:8-9).

50 BATTLE PLANS, PART 3: OVER THE TOP

When an invading army wanted to break into a walled city, it might build a siege mound. This was a big ramp made from dirt, mud, rocks, and debris. The army made the ramp bigger and bigger until it was tall enough to reach the top of the wall. Sometimes this took months. Then the invaders simply walked up and jumped over the wall and into the city. The Bible mentions siege mounds in Ezekiel 4:1-2 and Jeremiah 32:24.

Look, the siege mounds! They have come to the city to take it; and the city has been given into the hand of the Chaldeans (Jeremiah 32:24).

51 OUTGUNNED

According to 1 Samuel 13:19, the Philistines removed blacksmiths from Israel so that the Israelites couldn't make swords or spears. Only two people in all of Israel had swords or spears.

So it came about, on the day of battle, that there was neither sword nor spear found in the hand of any of the people who were with Saul and Jonathan. But they were found with Saul and Jonathan his son (1 Samuel 13:22).

CATCHPHRASE:
The Skin of our Teeth

When we say someone escaped by the skin of his teeth, we mean he barely made it. This comes from Job 19:20, which says the same thing happened to Job.

52 HOW TALL WAS GOLIATH?

We're not exactly sure how tall Goliath was. If a cubit was 18 inches and a span was approximately the width of a hand, Goliath would have been 9 feet, 9 inches tall. Some people think the cubit was 21 inches, and that would put him over 11 feet! The average NBA center is 7 feet tall, so Goliath and his four brothers (2 Samuel 21:22) would have made a great starting lineup.

And a champion went out from the camp of the Philistines, named Goliath, from Gath, whose height was six cubits and a span (1 Samuel 17:4).

53 THE SHEPHERD'S SLING

David's sling wasn't like our modern slingshots. It was a small leather patch with two long straps. After placing a rock in the patch, the shepherd held both straps and swung the sling over his head. When he let go of one of the straps, the stone would zing out at more than 60 miles an hour! A sharpshooting shepherd could hit a target 50 yards away.

Then David put his hand in his bag and took out a stone; and he slung it and struck the Philistine in his forehead (1 Samuel 17:49).

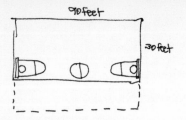

54 SOLOMON'S TEMPLE

Solomon's temple was 90 feet long and 30 feet wide. That's about as long as a basketball court but narrower. It wasn't a meeting place, so it didn't need to be very big. When the people came for a special festival, they gathered outside in the large courtyard.

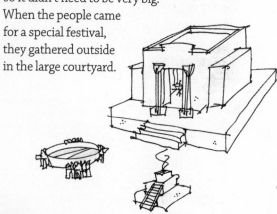

Now the house which King Solomon built for the LORD, its length was sixty cubits, its width twenty, and its height thirty cubits (1 Kings 6:2).

WORD 4 WORD:
Mediator (Greek, mesites)

This word combines two Greek words—*mesos* (middle) and *eimi* (to go). It describes someone in the middle, or as we would say, a middleman. It's like an umpire, or a mediator, someone who brings two parties together the way Jesus did for us and God (1 Timothy 2:5).

The ark of the covenant was different from
Noah's ark or the ark Moses floated in as a
baby. It was a beautiful chest covered with
gold that contained the stone tablets on which
God had written the Ten Commandments.
The ark rested beneath two carved winged
figures called cherubim. When the temple was
destroyed in 586 BC, the ark of the covenant
disappeared. Some people think it may still be
hidden in Jerusalem or elsewhere.

*And you shall make two cherubim of gold; of hammered
work you shall make them at the two ends of the mercy seat
(Exodus 25:18).*

56 JONAH'S JOURNEY

God spoke to Jonah and told him to go to
the wicked city of Nineveh and preach. Well,
Jonah hated the Ninevites and knew that
if they turned from their ways, God would
forgive them. And he didn't want that. So
Jonah took off in the opposite direction from
Nineveh, toward a city called Tarshish. But
God had different plans for Jonah.

*But Jonah arose to flee to Tarshish from the presence of the
LORD. He went down to Joppa, and found a ship going to
Tarshish (Jonah 1:3).*

57 KINDA FISHY

What kind of fish swallowed Jonah? No one
knows exactly. Many people speculate that
it was a great white shark. A 19-foot shark
can swallow a man whole. Large sperm
whales have also been known to visit the
Mediterranean. Sperm whales grow up to 65
feet long—plenty of room in there for Jonah.
Or it might have just been a really big fish.
Either way, the Bible says that God prepared
the fish especially to rescue Jonah.

*Now the LORD had prepared a great fish to swallow Jonah.
And Jonah was in the belly of the fish three days and three
nights (Jonah 1:17).*

58 FOR REAL?

Did Jonah really exist? Some people think this story is just a legend. (It is pretty incredible!) But Jonah was a real person. Second Kings 14:25 mentions him as a prophet during the reign of King Jeroboam II of Israel, and Jesus spoke of Jonah.

For as Jonah was three days and three nights in the belly of the great fish, so will the Son of Man be three days and three nights in the heart of the earth (Matthew 12:40).

59 CHECK IT OUT

The big fish wasn't the only thing that God sent Jonah's way. Read the story in the book of Jonah and see if you can find these four other things: a storm, a plant, a worm, and the east wind (1:4; 4:6-8).

But the LORD sent out a great wind on the sea, and there was a mighty tempest on the sea (Jonah 1:4).

WORD 4 WORD:
Offense (Greek, *skandalon*)

This word originally meant "a trap," like for an animal complete with bait. It describes something that might trick you and cause you to sin.

60 WHO DONE IT?

The book of Esther records one of the most beautiful stories in the whole Bible, but God is never mentioned in the entire book. Even so, you can't read it for too long without seeing His hand working behind the scenes. Our lives are often pretty much the same way, aren't they?

Yet who knows whether you have come to the kingdom for such a time as this? (Esther 4:14).

61 THE ROYAL CUPBEARER

The book of Nehemiah starts out in the country of Persia in the Middle East. At that time Nehemiah was serving as the cupbearer of the king. Part of Nehemiah's job was to taste the king's wine to make sure it wasn't poisoned. King Artaxerxes was extra-sensitive to this because his father had been assassinated.

Nehemiah isn't the only cupbearer in the Bible. In the book of Genesis, Joseph made friends with Pharoah's cupbearer while they both spent time in prison (Genesis 40).

"Let your servant prosper this day, I pray, and grant him mercy in the sight of this man." For I was the king's cupbearer (Nehemiah 1:11).

62 OFF THE WALL

The book of Nehemiah tells the story of the rebuilding of the wall around Jerusalem. In those days, for a city to be safe and secure, it needed a strong wall all the way around it. When Nehemiah arrived in Jerusalem, he saw that the walls had been completely destroyed and the city was vulnerable to attack.

The wall of Jerusalem is also broken down, and its gates are burned with fire (Nehemiah 1:3).

63 FEASTS AND FESTS, PART 1: THE PASSOVER

The most important festival of the year for
the Jewish people is Passover. This feast
celebrates the time God delivered His people
from slavery in Egypt. He sent ten plagues
against Egypt, and the final plague was the
death of the firstborn. But God told His
people to sacrifice a lamb and wipe some of
the blood over the doorposts of their houses.
When the angel of the Lord saw the blood,
he "passed over" that house, and the firstborn
didn't die. Jesus—the Lamb of God—was
crucified during the Passover celebration.

---

*Now the blood shall be a sign for you on the houses where
you are. And when I see the blood, I will pass over you; and
the plague shall not be on you to destroy you (Exodus 12:13).*

64 FEASTS AND FESTS, PART 2: THE FEAST OF TABERNACLES (OR BOOTHS)

At the end of September, the people of Israel held a feast to commemorate their journey through the wilderness. In the wilderness, the Jews had lived in tents, or "tabernacles." During this festival, all the people built booths made of branches and leaves and camped in them for a week in Jerusalem to remind them of that time. All week long during this feast, four large candelabras gave light to the whole city from the temple. This might have been when Jesus stood up and called Himself the light of the world.

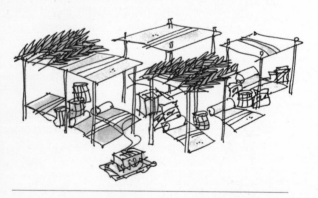

I am the light of the world. He who follows Me shall not walk in darkness, but have the light of life (John 8:12).

CATCHPHRASE:
A Wolf in Sheep's Clothing

In Matthew 7:15, Jesus warned His disciples to watch out for false prophets who look like sheep on the outside but inside are hungry wolves. Nowadays when we say this phrase, we mean someone who looks nice on the outside but has unhelpful thoughts inside.

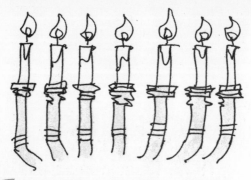

65 FEASTS AND FESTS, PART 3: HANUKAH

Hanukah, or the Festival of Lights, is a more recent celebration that isn't mentioned in the Bible. It occurs in December. During a time of struggle with Syria, a brave Jewish leader named Judas Maccabaeus led an army that drove the Syrians out of the land. Then he cleansed the temple because the Syrians had spoiled it. A legend says that when the Jews entered the temple, the lamp had only one day's supply of oil, but God miraculously kept the lamps burning for eight days. As a result, this festival lasts eight days. Jewish boys and girls often get a gift on each of those days. During this festival, many Jewish families light the menorah, a candelabra with seven branches, in remembrance of God's miracle.

WORD 4 WORD:
Power (Greek, *dunamis*)

This word denotes energy, power, might, and strength. It's also where we get the word *dynamite*. Jesus displayed great power (*dunamis*) wherever He went (Luke 4:14).

66 FEASTS AND FESTS, PART 4: THE DAY OF ATONEMENT

The Day of Atonement was the one day of the year when the high priest entered the most holy place in the temple to offer sacrifices to God on behalf of the people. But first, early in the morning, he killed one goat for a sacrifice. Then he laid his hand on a second goat's head, symbolically transferring the people's sins onto that animal. Then he sent it away into the wilderness forever. This is where the word *scapegoat* originated. It refers to someone who is blamed for something he didn't do.

But the goat on which the lot fell to be the scapegoat shall be presented alive before the LORD, to make atonement upon it, and to let it go as the scapegoat into the wilderness (Leviticus 16:10).

67 SLOW GOING

Mary and Joseph probably walked the 80 miles from Nazareth to Bethlehem. The trip would have taken them a week or more because Mary was nine months pregnant. Today you could make this trip in less than two hours by car.

Joseph also went up from Galilee, out of the city of Nazareth, into Judea, to the city of David, which is called Bethlehem, because he was of the house and lineage of David, to be registered with Mary, his betrothed wife, who was with child (Luke 2:4-5).

68 ROOM FOR TWO, PLEASE

Did you know that the inn that Mary and Joseph were turned away from was most likely an upstairs room of someone's house? It might have even belonged to Joseph's relative. The word that Luke uses for *inn* is the same Greek word he uses for the upper room where the disciples shared the Last Supper with Jesus.

While they were there, the days were completed for her to be delivered...There was no room for them in the inn (Luke 2:6-7).

69 WAY AWAY IN A MANGER

In Jesus' time, people sometimes kept farm animals in caves near the village rather than in wooden barns like we imagine. The manger was just a feeding trough that held hay and grains for the larger animals to eat. Sometimes a newborn lamb would be placed in the manger to keep it warm. Jesus, the Lamb of God, slept there too.

She brought forth her firstborn son, and wrapped Him in swaddling cloths, and laid Him in a manger (Luke 2:7).

WORD 4 WORD:
Repent (Greek, *metanoeo*)

This word combines two words—*meta* (after) and *noeo* (to think). It means "to make a choice to change your thinking." And new thinking often leads to changed actions and habits (Luke 15:7).

70 BABY SHOWER

The gifts the wise men brought were very expensive—especially to be given to a poor family like Mary and Joseph and Jesus. Gold was a sign of royalty. Frankincense was used to make incense for the temple. It was made from the gummy resin of a tree grown in Arabia. People made cuts in the tree and drained the resin out, a lot like when people tap trees for maple syrup today. And myrrh was a perfume that scented the holy anointing oil. John 19:39 mentions that Nicodemus prepared a mixture of myrrh and aloes to anoint Jesus' body after He was crucified.

And when they had come into the house, they saw the young Child with Mary His mother, and fell down and worshiped Him. And when they had opened their treasures, they presented gifts to Him: gold, frankincense, and myrrh (Matthew 2:11).

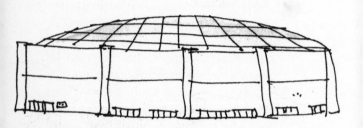

71 URBAN SPRAWL

Jerusalem grew a lot from the time of David to the time of Jesus. When David lived in Jerusalem, it was so small it could have fit inside the Louisiana Superdome, with room to spare!

Then David dwelt in the stronghold, and called it the City of David (2 Samuel 5:9).

72 CAPERNAUM

The Gospels record many of Jesus' miracles, including 18 that occurred along the shores of the Sea of Galilee. Ten of these were done in the little seaside town of Capernaum, which is where Jesus healed the paralyzed man who was lowered through a roof by his four friends. In fact, that might have happened in Peter's house!

And leaving Nazareth, He came and dwelt in Capernaum, which is by the sea, in the regions of Zebulun and Naphtali (Matthew 4:13).

INSTANT STORMS

The Sea of Galilee is a great spot for the perfect storm. It sits on an earthquake fault line, its elevation is 690 feet below sea level, and it rests between high hills on both sides. As a result, violent storms often brew without warning. The mountains act like a wind tunnel, driving the air currents down their slopes and onto the water. The Gospels mention that two of these storms caught the disciples by surprise.

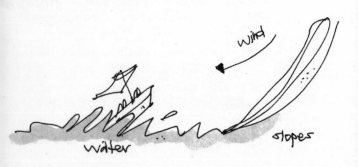

And a windstorm came down on the lake, and they were filling with water, and were in jeopardy (Luke 8:23).

74 CATCH OF THE DAY

Jesus and Peter needed to pay their taxes but evidently didn't have any money. So Jesus told Peter to cast a hook into the water. Peter caught a fish—probably a tilapia. This kind of fish usually keeps its babies in its mouth. But when the mom needs a break, she picks up a shiny object and holds it in her mouth as a gate to keep the babies out. The fish that Peter caught had picked up a coin—just the right coin to pay the temple tax for Peter and Jesus.

Go to the sea, cast in a hook, and take the fish that comes up first. And when you have opened its mouth, you will find a piece of money (Matthew 17:27).

WORD 4 WORD:
Save (Greek, sozo)

This word has a variety of meanings: to save, heal, cure, rescue, or deliver. It can also mean "to give new life" (1 Timothy 1:8-9).

75 IT'S A MIRACLE!

In Bible times, leprosy was a terrible disease. It caused numbness, deformity, and major skin problems. People thought it was highly contagious, so lepers weren't allowed to touch anyone. In fact, they had to live outside the city. Whenever they came near anyone, they had to shout out "Unclean!" so everyone would stay clear. But Jesus wasn't afraid to be near lepers. He healed several of them of their painful disease.

Then Jesus put out His hand and touched him, saying, "I am willing; be cleansed." Immediately his leprosy was cleansed (Matthew 8:3).

Jesus healed people on the Sabbath even though the religious leaders disapproved. How many Sabbath healings occur in the Gospels? Seven. In two of those accounts, the healed person was a woman, and in the other five, the healed person was a man.

Then Jesus said to them, "I will ask you one thing: Is it lawful on the Sabbath to do good or to do evil, to save life or to destroy?" (Luke 6:9).

77 FISH FRY

A young boy gave Jesus five flat biscuits and two fish, and Jesus used that little bit of food to feed 5000 hungry men and the women and children with them—perhaps ten thousand people in all. Even if each person ate only half of what the boy brought for himself, Jesus miraculously provided 25,000 loaves of bread and 10,000 fish! And it all started when the boy gave all he had. This miracle is one of the few that is reported in all four Gospels.

There is a lad here who has five barley loaves and two small fish, but what are they among so many? (John 6:9).

CATCHPHRASE:
The Handwriting on the Wall

When someone says he sees the handwriting on the wall, he means he sees trouble ahead. In Daniel 5, King Belshazzar saw mysterious writing appear on his palace wall. Daniel interpreted it and it foretold the king's downfall.

78 MESSIAH

Messiah means "anointed one." In Old Testament times, as people poured oil on the priests and kings God had chosen, God poured the Holy Spirit on them to give them the power they needed to do their jobs. God hinted that one day He would send a Messiah—an anointed one—to establish His kingdom on earth.

The Greek word for *Messiah* is *Christos*, so when we say "Jesus Christ," we're saying "Jesus the Messiah" or "Jesus the Anointed One."

Simon Peter answered and said, "You are the Christ, the Son of the living God" (Matthew 16:16).

79 PALM SUNDAY

When Jesus made His triumphal entry into Jerusalem, the people cheered for Him and shouted things like "Hosanna! Save now!" quoting from Psalm 118:25. They waved palm branches as if they were welcoming a king. These branches came from the date palm trees that grew nearby. Date palms grow to about 90 feet and have branches 9 feet long. People not only ate the dates but also made roofing material from the branches, camel feed from the seeds, and rope from the crowns.

When they heard that Jesus was coming to Jerusalem, [they] took branches of palm trees and went out to meet Him, and cried out: "Hosanna! Blessed is He who comes in the name of the LORD!" (John 12:12-13).

WORD 4 WORD:
Spirit (Hebrew, ruach)

This is an interesting word because it can mean "spirit," "breath," or "wind." Most of the time it means "spirit," but the word is used to describe windy storms and even the breath of life that fills all the creatures God has created (Genesis 6:17).

80 FIT FOR A KING

In wartime, a conquering king rode into his new city on a big, powerful horse. But if he came in peace, he rode on a donkey. Jesus was coming in peace and reconciliation, so He too rode a donkey. This had been predicted 400 years earlier by the prophet Zechariah.

Behold, your King is coming to you; He is just and having salvation, lowly and riding on a donkey, a colt, the foal of a donkey (Zechariah 9:9).

81 | THE LAST SUPPER, PART 1: RECLINING AT THE TABLE

When the disciples joined Jesus for the Last Supper, they didn't sit on chairs at a table the way we do. They reclined on the floor and propped themselves up on one elbow. The Passover was usually celebrated this way because in ancient times, this is how people who weren't slaves ate their meals. This posture reminded the people that God had set them free.

When the hour had come, He reclined at the table, and the apostles with Him (Luke 22:14 NASB).

82 THE LAST SUPPER, PART 2: FOUR CUPS

Four cups of wine were used in the Passover meal. When Jesus said one cup represented the new covenant, He was referring to the cup that symbolized redemption. Jesus redeemed us by paying the price for our sins on the cross.

This cup is the new covenant in My blood, which is shed for you (Luke 22:20).

During the meal, three pieces of unleavened bread were kept in a special container. Two pieces of the bread were eaten, but one was hidden until the end of the meal. When Jesus broke the bread and said, "This is My body," He was telling the disciples that He was going to be separated from the Father and the Holy Spirit. He would be broken and brought back to life.

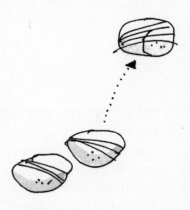

And He took bread, gave thanks and broke it, and gave it to them, saying, "This is My body which is given for you; do this in remembrance of Me" (Luke 22:19).

84 THE LAST SUPPER, PART 4: THE LAMB OF GOD

Remember the Passover lamb? (See Awesome Bible Fact 63.) The lamb eaten in the Passover meal represented the blood spread on doorways to protect families from the angel of death during the Exodus. When Jesus died, He took the place of the Passover lamb forever.

Then they shall eat the flesh on that night; roasted in fire, with unleavened bread and with bitter herbs they shall eat it (Exodus 12:8).

WORD 4 WORD:
Strong (Hebrew, *chazaq*)

This word means "strong, courageous, established, firm, and mighty." It also can refer to being encouraged, as in being strengthened by the Lord or others.

85 HE DiED FOR YOU

At the moment Jesus died, something incredible was happening at the temple. The curtain that separated the most holy place from the rest of the temple was torn in two from top to bottom. The Jewish historian Josephus reports that the curtain was about four inches thick and so strong that a pair of horses couldn't pull it apart. But God tore it apart at that very second to show that people were no longer separated from Him. We can go into God's presence anytime and all the time through Jesus!

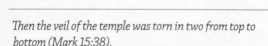

Then the veil of the temple was torn in two from top to bottom (Mark 15:38).

86 THE CROWN

When the soldiers wove a crown of thorns
to crush down on Jesus' head, they probably
used a bush that is now called Christ's-thorn.
The plant has extremely long, sharp thorns—
much longer than rosebush thorns.

*And they clothed Him with purple; and they twisted a
crown of thorns, put it on His head, and began to salute
Him, "Hail, King of the Jews!" (Mark 15:17-18).*

87 THE CROSS

Crucifixion was one of the most brutal and cruel forms of execution. It was invented by the Assyrians. (Remember Jonah?) The prisoner was either nailed or tied to the cross. Often his feet reached down to a peg, which reduced the pressure on his arms and prolonged his agony. In order to gasp a quick breath, the prisoner had to push up on his feet to relax the chest cavity. To make sure the prisoner had died, they broke his legs so he could no longer push up, and he suffocated. The soldiers didn't break Jesus' legs because He had already "given up His spirit."

For these things were done that the Scripture should be fulfilled, "Not one of His bones shall be broken" (John 19:36).

He guards all his bones; not one of them is broken (Psalm 34:20).

88 HE IS RISEN! PART 1: THE FAMILY PLOT

The tomb Jesus was placed in wasn't a hole in the ground. It was more like a cave. It was carved out of one of the limestone hills that surrounded Jerusalem. Each tomb had several chambers, depending on how many people were in the family. The stone in front of the tomb was shaped like a large, heavy wheel. It sealed the tomb but could be rolled away later.

When Joseph [of Arimathea] had taken the body, he wrapped it in a clean linen cloth, and laid it in his new tomb which he had hewn out of the rock; and he rolled a large stone against the door of the tomb (Matthew 27:59-60).

89 HE IS RISEN! PART 2: JESUS' BODY

When Jesus first appeared after rising from the dead, the disciples were understandably afraid. They thought He was a ghost, but He wasn't. They saw their friend and Lord in a new, glorified state. Look at the cool things He could now do:

1 He could appear and disappear whenever He wanted.

2 He could show up wherever He wanted, even in a room with a locked door.

3 He could still be recognized (most of the time) because He had a real body, complete with scars from the cross.

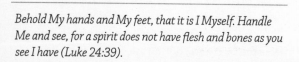

4 He could eat food. He ate broiled fish with the disciples to show them He was real.

Behold My hands and My feet, that it is I Myself. Handle Me and see, for a spirit does not have flesh and bones as you see I have (Luke 24:39).

WORD 4 WORD:
Word (Greek, rhema)

This term refers to a spoken word, as opposed to *logos*, which usually refers to the expression of a thought or message. Paul uses the word *rhema* in Ephesians 6:17 when he says that we're to use the word (*rhema*) of God as a sword for protection and warfare.

90 CAREER DAY, PART 1: THE SHEPHERD

People made their living in many ways in Jesus' day. Israel was full of farmers, bankers, physicians, and merchants. There were seamstresses, weavers, potters, and of course shepherds and fishermen.

A shepherd carried a staff that was usually about six feet long. He used it to guide the sheep. He also carried a rod—a small club to fight off wild animals. David mentions the rod and staff in Psalm 23. Most shepherds kept their food and supplies in a leather bag, or *scrip*.

For You are with me; Your rod and Your staff, they comfort me (Psalm 23:4).

CATCHPHRASE:
An Eye for an Eye

An eye for an eye means paying someone back for something he did to you in the same measure (Exodus 21:24). But Jesus said we should never return evil for evil, but to learn to forgive instead.

CAREER DAY. PART 2: NiGHT FiSHiNG

Before Peter, Andrew, James, and John met Jesus, they worked as fishermen. Most fishing was done at night. Fishermen used torches to draw the fish to the surface. Then they pulled long nets through the water to collect their catch.

But Simon answered and said to Him, "Master, we have toiled all night and caught nothing; nevertheless at Your word I will let down the net" (Luke 5:5).

BIBLE BONUS:
Paul's Journeys

On Paul's three missionary journeys around the Mediterranean, he traveled more than 9200 miles. That's like walking, riding a donkey, and sailing on a ship from Canada to the tip of South Africa!

92 THE PASSWORD

Early Christians used the symbol of a fish like a secret code. When *fish* is spelled in the Greek language, its letters form the initials of the phrase "Jesus Christ, God's Son, Savior."

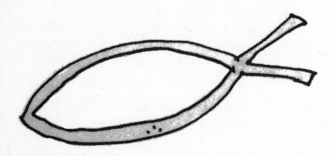

We ourselves have heard Him and we know that this indeed is the Christ, the Savior of the world (John 4:42).

93 THE ROMANS, PART 1: ORGANIZING THE TROOPS

Israel was under Roman occupation while Jesus was on earth. Rome was the most powerful nation in the world at that time. Just as modern armies have platoons and companies, the Roman army was divided into smaller units:

1 century (a centurion commanded a century of men)—100 men

2 centuries (200 men)—1 maniple

3 maniples (600 men)—1 cohort

10 cohorts (6000 men)—1 legion

When the centurion, who stood opposite Him, saw that He cried out like this and breathed His last, he said, "Truly this Man was the Son of God!" (Mark 15:39).

94 THE ROMANS, PART 2: A PORTABLE MISSILE LAUNCHER

One of the most powerful war engines in ancient times was the catapult. It could fling a whole bunch of javelins at enemy soldiers or hurl boulders against city walls, cracking them and sometimes even breaking all the way through. Some catapults could throw a 100-pound stone, and some could shoot a boulder almost half a mile. In AD 66, a commander named Titus laid siege against Jerusalem. He pounded the walls with catapults for three and a half years before he finally broke through.

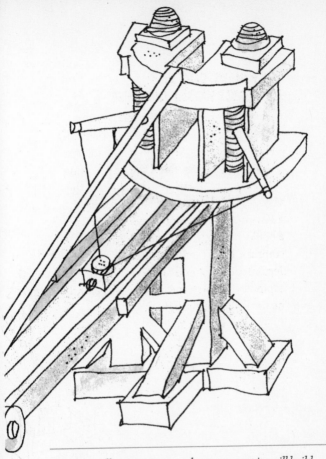

For days will come upon you when your enemies will build an embankment around you, surround you and close you in on every side (Luke 19:43).

WORD 4 WORD:
Worship (Greek, *proskuneo*)

This word means "to bow down, show reverence, worship, or adore." As we follow Jesus, we learn the importance and power of worship, not just on Sundays but all the time.

Let's see.... helmet of salvation, breastplate of righteousness, belt of truth...

95 THE ROMANS, PART 3: BODY ARMOR

A Roman soldier was equipped with a large shield, a breastplate, and a helmet made of metal or leather. When the apostle Paul wrote to the Ephesian church about Christian warfare, he was probably guarded by a Roman soldier. When he described the breastplate of righteousness, the shield of faith, the helmet of salvation, and the sword of the Spirit, he could have been looking right at the soldier's armor.

Stand therefore, having girded your waist with truth, having put on the breastplate of righteousness, and having shod your feet with the preparation of the gospel of peace; above all, taking the shield of faith...the helmet of salvation, and the sword of the Spirit, which is the word of God (Ephesians 6:14-17).

96 THE PHARISEES

Three main groups dominated the religious scene in Israel in Jesus' time: the Pharisees, the Sadducees, and the Herodians. The Pharisees were mostly middle-class working people who started out trying to follow God and His commandments. But they went too far. They developed extra rules, or "oral traditions," to make sure people wouldn't break the Mosaic law. The Pharisees were often guilty of sin but too proud to realize or admit it. Jesus had harsh words for some Pharisees.

He answered and said to [the scribes and Pharisees], "Why do you also transgress the commandment of God because of your tradition?" (Matthew 15:3).

97 THE SADDUCEES

Most of the Sadducees were wealthy land-owners. They had a lot of religious influence, but they were not very popular with the common people. The Sadducees were very strict about keeping the law, but they didn't believe in most of the Old Testament, angels, or the resurrection. Jesus made a special point mentioning angels and the resurrection when He answered the Sadducees.

But concerning the resurrection of the dead, have you not read what was spoken to you by God, saying, "I am the God of Abraham, the God of Isaac, and the God of Jacob"? God is not the God of the dead, but of the living (Matthew 22:31-32).

The Herodians were a less important group around Jerusalem at that time. They got their name because of their loyalty to King Herod and his sons. Even though the Romans occupied the land, they allowed King Herod to rule Israel. Normally the Herodians and the Pharisees didn't see eye to eye, but when Jesus arrived on the scene, they became united against Him.

Then the Pharisees went out and immediately plotted with the Herodians against Him, how they might destroy Him (Mark 3:6).

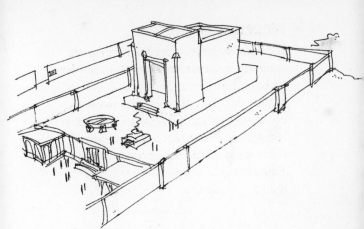

99 HEROD'S TEMPLE

King Herod was originally from Moab,
Israel's neighbor to the east. Because of
this, many of the Jewish people didn't trust
Herod. To win their favor, he expanded the
temple in Jerusalem and made it into a
magnificent place of worship. Jesus visited
the temple often.

*Now it happened on one of those days, as He taught the
people in the temple and preached the gospel, that the chief
priests and the scribes, together with the elders, confronted
Him (Luke 20:1).*

100 ALL ROADS LEAD TO ROME

The Roman road system was the best in the world. It connected Rome to Europe, Egypt, and beyond. Because of these advanced roads, Paul, Silas, Timothy, and many others spread the gospel throughout the civilized world. God used the Roman Empire's achievements to further His kingdom.

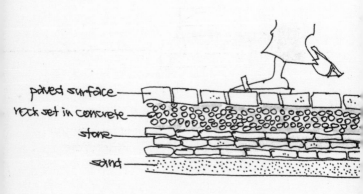

paved surface — rock set in concrete — stone — sand

While Apollos was at Corinth, Paul took the road through the interior and arrived at Ephesus (Acts 19:1 NIV).

101 WORTH A LOT

In the Middle Ages, a copy of the Bible cost more to produce than two arches of the London bridge!

The judgments of the LORD are true and righteous altogether. More to be desired are they than gold, yea, than much fine gold (Psalm 19:9-10).